BUBBLES TO CONCEPT

Urban Planning Made Easy—
A Design Guide for
Urban Planning and Architecture

Jerome Ezeanonye Nwokeji

Strategic Book Group

Strategic Book Group
P.O. Box 333
Durham CT 06422
www.StrategicBookClub.com

ISBN: 978-1-60976-851-5

Book Design: Suzanne Kelly

In loving memory of my late dear parents
Mr . Desmond Anonyuo Nwokeji
and
Mrs. Maria Anyatoroigbo Nwokeji

May all Glory and thanks be to God now and forever

TABLE OF CONTENTS

An Overview

The professional fields of Architecture, Landscape Architecture, and Urban Design and Planning are rooted and joined as one—that is, four in one—to a common rhythm at different frequencies. They have always existed in history, though initially without classification, and were gradually acknowledged and branded over the course of time.

Man has always designed shelter over his head, and the need for shelter necessitated taming the environment around him. We know from recorded history that he has always lived in communes, or clusters of settlements, which were arranged according to the best understandings of the time for effective farming and the efficient movement of people.

The advent of industrialization placed even greater demands on man's environment, and required even more effective planning and patterns to allow for the easy flow of goods and people. This resulted in a greater awareness of needs that had always existed, and resulted in the formal emergence of Architecture, Landscape Architecture, and Urban Design and Planning.

For effective and orderly creations, the four key elements of habitat development must be seen from a common overarching vision, with each firmly attached to the others and drawing inspiration from one another. They are each similar in many ways, and the success of each is derived from an understanding of the common values anchored in a proper interpretation of the whole endeavor.

In planning and design, a "vision" is first captured in a "master brief." The brief, in its broadest sense, is an aggregation of requirements that a designer must accomplish. The brief may be anything from a single page to a voluminous set of documents. When fully developed, it typically includes relevant needs, opportunities, constraints, and points for further investigation.

The urgent need for the proper interpretation and conceptualization of a brief to blend with available time necessitated the drive for this book, *"Bubbles to Concept: Urban Planning Made Easy—A Design Guide for Urban Planning and Architecture."*

The problem most designers encounter in the process of conceptualizing a brief is the challenge of translating the brief into a unique design, specifically tailored to satisfy the time and needs of the client(s) involved. In process of this, however, many designers do not realize that the client(s) they work with are often not the sole owner(s) of a brief. This is because the proposal will ultimately have direct or indirect impact on a great many other people within and beyond the jurisdiction of the proposed development.

Therefore, this book will present some relevant development and interpretation formulas derived from many years of professional practice. They are also rooted in an apprenticeship, in 1982, to Professor Richard Millar, who was an apprentice to Frank Lloyd Wright in 1958. Finally, case studies developed and expanded over the years will also be used to guide in urban-planning-architecture-designs/formulations.

The techniques presented are derived from overlooked, abandoned, and previously never imagined theorems, along with many others that will be revived, as well as old tenets reformulated to inform and guide the design process. Creativity will be harnessed by applying the guiding principles, uniquely tailored to accommodate the time allotted to satisfy the client's needs. The process of brief creation and interpretation will be systematically transformed, by going through the basic and fundamental techniques of conceptualization.

The process presented is unique, in that it will help a planner or designer to rediscover his architectural talents and to assume a new found confidence in leadership of his profession, understanding that he can actually be a master of originality. In other words, the process presented is a master key to the fundamental techniques of urban planning and architecture.

As a quality confidence enhancer, good "think tank" formulas will be presented, as developed from the original and basic theorems of essential design tactics.

CHAPTER 1

INTRODUCTION

INSPIRATION FROM NATURE

A true understanding of the evolutionary processes of living things in multiplying their kind is actually a key to creative inspiration. It is the stepping stone to unveiling the intrigues of emulating nature to access the fundamental secrets and great concepts that aid in creative development for today and tomorrow.

The guide to focused reasoning is best understood when comparative analysis is derived from the activities, actions, and patterns of life, and from the developmental stages of living things. An example derived from the life cycle of the Anopheles mosquito is illustrated below:

> *"Eggs—After mating, the Anopheles mosquito lays its eggs individually on the surface of stagnant water. After about one or two days, the eggs hatch into larva."*

> *"Lava—The Larva has nine segments and two (2) small brushes for drawing food particles into the mouth. The Larva (wriggler) of the Anopheles has [a] breathing siphon with valves on the 8th segment and gills at the 9th segment. The Larva lies horizontal to the water's surface and rests at an angle on a vertical surface. The head hangs down. It sinks down and wriggles upward in water. Within a period of 2 to about 14 days it moults 3 to 4 times and reaches a maximum size. After the last moult, it becomes a Pupa."*

"Pupa (Active Stage)—The pupa has a narrow abdomen with a tail fin and two respiratory trumpets for breathing. It remains in the pupal stage for a few hours to a few days [after which] the imago emerges".[1]

It is always good to backtrack a little, in other to achieve a good flow in both the present and future drive for understanding. In doing so, your first reaction may be to conclude that we have diverted on a tangent into another subject which does not have any relationship to our current study. However, it is very important for us to understand that nature, and its natural actions and actualities, are our greatest teacher. By observing how things are achieved naturally, we open our minds to questions that may readily lead to discovery.

It is normal to wonder about the relationship between the tiny "Anopheles mosquito" and the practice of urban planning. A careful and well articulated reasoning may help us to better understand the analogy. First, the mating of the male and female mosquito did not result in the automatic reproduction of a baby mosquito. No, after mating comes several precursor processes, namely: eggs—larva—pupa—imago—finally resulting in a brand new mosquito that has the qualities and characteristics of the parents.

We can re-create our own developmental stages by drawing a comparative analogy, both in thought and action flow, with the stages of the development of the Anopheles mosquito. A good, creative artist is never constrained by his pencils, but rather allows his hand to be the instrument to keep the pencil standing on the paper or on the board. In this way the designer allows the pencil to move freely without predetermining its actions completely.

In this process, it is important not to presume in the mind what is needed on the paper. Instead, let the movement of the pencil and the hand combine with underlying thoughts to more naturally devise the outcome of the action. The mating of the two tiny adult mosquitoes was necessitated in the first place by a natural drive to satisfy a desire or urge to have a fullness of each other. In much the same way, the mating of the mind, hand, pencil, and paper can result in a fruitful creative process.

Eggs

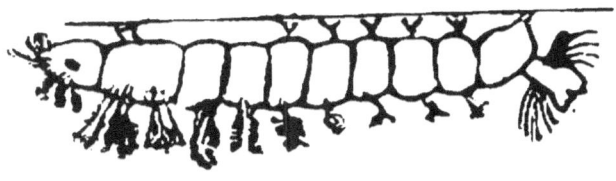

Larva

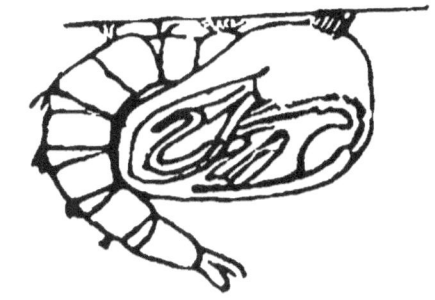

Pupa

Adult

FIGURE 1
Stages in the life cycle of an Anopheles mosquito

Remember, however, that the mating in nature was not intended to immediately result in completely developed off-spring. Rather, the coupling event activated a process that continued through multiple stages to achieve its final unique result, which is, a brand new mosquito. A careful look at the stages of development in their natural forms will reveal a flow of variations that are not pre-determined, but rather programmed to achieve a final result—a new mosquito.

Similarly, a desire by a client to commission a consultant for a design to satisfy a need should trigger a mutually creative flow. It should culminate in the fulfillment of the dreams of both the client and the consultant.

Before we get into the actual business of designing, let us examine another good example that is very close to us: the development of humans. This second example will further unveil the various gifts of nature to humanity and aid in awakening our creative imagination. The life cycle of humans from conception to birth is detailed below:

> *"[T]he egg or ovum [is] fertilized in the oviduct [and] forms a zygote which attaches itself to the uterus wall and begins to grow and develop by cell division to form an embryo. The foetus or embryo obtains oxygen and food from the mother's blood through the placenta and also waste products from the embryo pass into the mother's blood through the placenta.*

> *It takes about nine (9) months for the embryo to be fully grown and [it] is born thereafter. The period from fertilization to birth is called the gestation period".*[2]

The two examples provided, involving the reproductive analyses of the Anopheles mosquito and humans, as illustrated in Figures 1 and 2, reveal important and useful understandings. They demonstrate not only the natural flow of activities or actions that triggered the reproduction of their kinds, but they also expose the artistic, natural, bubbling flow that we can emulate to produce our own "bubbles" of creativity.

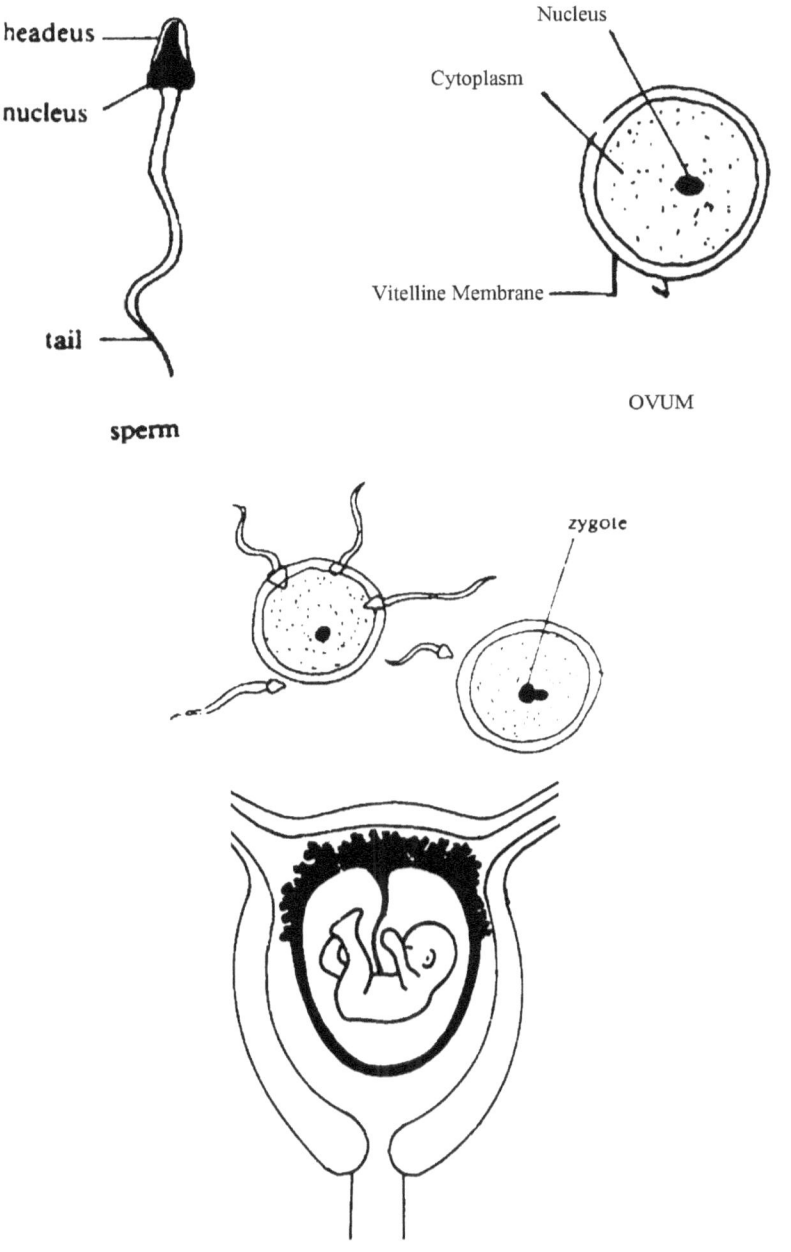

FIGURE 2
Development of fertilized ovum in humans

We have observed that the bubbles in the reproductive processes are progressive—that is, they change and improve at each
stage. The creative bubbles continuously bubble along at every
level until they arrived at a unique form and an accepted final
outcome. One thing is very obvious: something triggered the
bubbling processes. In nature, it was the urge or desire of two
adult creatures to engage in the creative (reproductive) process.
In our case the client(s) has a need and desires a consultant to
realize or satisfy a similarly creative dream.

The client's brief and his search for a good consultant both
represent the desire to accomplish a dream. For his part, the
consultant is anxious to showcase his talent and generate a
livelihood from his professional practice. Therefore, he desires
a quality client. At this point a union is created between the two
parties which will now activate a similar process of creative
flow, as can be seen in our reproductive examples in Figures 1
and 2. The end result of a designer's creative bubbles should be
a materialization of creative ingenuity, even like that conceived
and carried out in nature.

CHAPTER 2

UNDERSTANDING BUBBLES

The principles and theorems of "bubbles" as idea developers were learned from the free flowing natural activities of animals, and from our own daily actions. Both serve to awaken our thinking faculties to realize that we can achieve great results by emulating nature.

Bubbles can be activated by our actions just as bubbles actively emerge in nature. Examples include bubbles springing out from soap, foaming and gradually breaking into many smaller bubbles; or, a tiny ball of air or gas produced in a liquid or solid, such as in carbonated water or in glass, etc. Bubbles have unique and similar characteristics, including the ability to expand, diminish, multiply, cluster in multiplication, and vanish into another state or form. It is very useful to understand the true nature of bubbles, as in soap foaming into multiples of bubbles. Bubbles don't have a particular or pre-determined pattern. Thus, in other words, their flow is unpredictable and endlessly "creative."

Using soap bubbles as an illustration will enable us understand the characteristics of bubbles and how we can derive knowledge from the uniqueness of bubbles. The soap-foam bubbles flow, float, dangle, and multiply in continuity, and the speed of their movement is determined by numerous factors including air pressure. As bubbles are created, they form different sizes and different clusters. Some are linked to their original sources, while others may be completely detached from the source. Some may lose the grip of its nature before vanishing into another state or form, while others will vanish without losing their original form.

A good observational study of soap foam and its bubbles and bubble behavior will help further awaken our reasoning and understanding about how and why bubbles can be used for conceptualization.

Going a little further, similar comparative analyses between natural activities and actions—as shown in Figure 1 and 2 for the life cycle of the Anopheles mosquito, plus the development of fertilized ova in humans—can generate an analytical relationship between natural phenomena and insinuated actions. Consider, for example, how the soap foaming into bubbles can trigger an awareness of the value of artistic bubbles for concept creation.

Understanding bubbles and bubbling can produce strategic skills for effective design development for Urban Designers and Planners, architects and landscape architects, and in fact for all creative design professionals.

Indeed, the greatest tool a designer can obtain is the acquisition of bubbles and bubbling skills and the ability to use the bubbles effectively. Bubbles and Bubbling are natural phenomena, which if understood, are wonderful skills for any creative designer to utilize.

CHAPTER 3

BRIEF TAKING

When a designer is first approached, the client brings a dream and a set of ideas of what he desires with him. He may also have researched and traveled far and near to package his desires into a brief. The accompanying desires may be a culmination of imaginations, or even wild thoughts in great fantasies. Regardless, the client is constantly imagining a day when those ideas will come to fulfillment. The ideas could be gathered from consultations far and near, several organized meetings, interviews conducted for opinion gathering and enhancement, and/or case studies of similar projects to discover more about the pros and cons of the project in formulation.

The compiled documentation of these investigations, analyses, thoughts and ideas in written, graphic, or photographic format forms the client's brief. Armed with the brief, the client will now need the services of a consultant or groups of consultants to translate his ideas into reality.

The consultant, at this stage, should contribute toward the harmonization of the brief. He must come to understand in clear terms the ideas, reasoning, purposes, and dreams in the client's brief. Otherwise, he may not properly capture the intensions of the brief.

Understanding the client's brief is crucial. One must not assume an understanding of a master brief, even as presented by the client at the outset. Instead, become a good friend to the client and be skilled listener. Take the client down "memory lane," as related to the contents of the brief, before arriving at the desired level of the brief. One by one, item by item, discuss it, evaluate it, and table each element for subsequent conference analysis by all involved. In this way, common agreement can be achieved even while gradually introducing your professional guidance in every evaluative stage of the brief.

Brief taking is a very important stage. If it is not well evaluated and understood, the end result will not be satisfactory to both parties. Therefore, this level of analysis is very critical and even essential for a proper project launch. Otherwise, it will be an exercise destined to fail.

In order to create a good atmosphere for proper comprehension by all involved, trips to visit similar projects may be arranged. These will enhance evaluation process. Opinion interviews of past clients and other end-users may be organized, and random sampling may also be obtained to help in statistical development and to round out the brief properly.

When a good understanding of all the information needed is clear, and when it has been jointly agreed upon by all parties, a catalogue of the relevant information will be formulated and compiled by the consultant. The comprehensive document must now encompass the client's intensions, and it must be produced in both hard and soft copies. The data must then be rolled out for all to agree upon the details as compiled. Only then can it be assumed that the brief is complete and ready to be prepared by the consultant. The final document must also be approved, signed, and distributed to all parties concerned with the project.

BRIEF TRANSLATION

Translating the client's brief into a consultancy assignment is a major test of comprehension for any professional. At this stage, the ideas of the client must be plotted into a diagnostic format for the expert to understand the critical conditions and begin to imagine solutions.

Translation can actually be readily accomplished if the brief is well understood. Otherwise, it will be like trying to translate a language you do not understand. The key at this point is a complete understanding of all the information as related to the client(s). The expert is like a language translator for the client(s), and the brief at this point is the language that needs to be translated into a version that is comprehensible to the owner(s)/end-users. They must be seen as the listeners or the audience that ultimately need to hear the story or information. This explains why the consultant must be the master of the brief. Otherwise, sooner or later it will become clear that a problem is at hand. Just as a wrong diagnosis will lead to the beginning of bad treatment for any illness, the obvious result or consequence is certain.

Translation, at this level, is intended to expand all the items of the brief. Additional research is needed on all the elements in the document, and drawing upon the various case studies will put the consultant on top of his assignment. Translation is the second job of the expert, and that is the reason why he must master the brief in his own language. Precisely how to master a brief is a key question. It will uncover the way forward at this level of the assignment.

To become the master of a brief is an enormous task. It calls for intensive information gathering to enhance the knowledge of the client's intention, as handed over to the consultant in confidence—and with a fee attached. Therefore, the client deserves the best. We must see the brief as a language and the professional as the interpreter standing in front of a large audience. The crowd is depending on the interpreter to translate the language and communicate it to them.

BRIEF ANALYSIS

The brief translation should flow naturally into "analysis"—that is, breaking down, re-organizing, re-integrating, and gradually formatting the brief into another stage of the conceptualization level of design.

The first stage, as already discussed, was client/consultant fusion. This stage was compared to the attraction of two Anopheles mosquitoes, plus the additional comparison regarding the sexual desire of two adult humans. The second stage (Brief Taking) was compared to the mating of the Anopheles mosquitoes and the sexual union of two adult humans, which naturally triggered a process that eventually resulted in the reproduction of their respective kinds.

Similarly, the desire of the client to accomplish his dream led to the appointment of a consultant, which resulted in brief taking, and now leads to brief analysis. This should ultimately trigger the commencement of an analysis in creative bubbles that will eventually flow into formal conceptualization.

Unquestionably, a designer can only analyze and translate a brief properly if the picture of the assignment is very clear. In other words, you must have a very good knowledge or understanding of the brief. That explains the reason why a thorough job must be done during the translation stage. In the analysis stage, each section of the brief should be detailed and organized into a flow chart that identifies key "functional relationships."

Functional relationships help identify the need for proximity, use, activities, patterns, and the nature of all sections. Attending to functional relationships can enhance their arrangement for groupings, systematic alignments, and actions flow. Actions in the various sections should be identified and analyzed into one flow, or perhaps into double or multiple flow patterns if needed to facilitate the adequate arrangement of spaces.

BRIEF PROGRAMMING

Once we are on top of our assignment and have achieved a good analysis, the functional relationships and related actions will flow naturally into "brief programming."

Brief programming is much more than the term itself implies. In this stage, the designer must understand the programming process before the concept can be applied to further enhance the brief. In simple terms, brief programming refers to putting the already translated and analyzed information in the brief into a unique, transitional format. In this format it is prepared to be interpreted or decoded into another creative stage. The decoding process will better aid the consultant to understand and enable a continues flow of the brief to the next level on the conceptualization ladder.

Programming includes formatting the analyzed brief, and then arranging, organizing, distributing, and harmonizing all sections. Quality programming guarantees that the relationships of spaces, functions, and forms will be properly interwoven.

It is at this stage that we must achieve essential orderliness. This requires a good sequence of spatial relationships, proximity relationships, horizontal and vertical relationships, interlocking relationships, visual relationships, and a final harmony of all spaces and needs as contained in the translated and analyzed brief.

BRIEF GROUPINGS

Now that the designer is armed with a complete program derived from the brief, the stage is set for the groupings of the details of the program. Again the arrangement of spaces will be easy if quality programming was achieved.

The section groupings should be based on the information already gathered, and the groupings must be anchored in key guiding principles, such as functionality, necessity, dependability, use, and values, as well as past, present, and future projections.

BRIEF GROUP RELATIONSHIPS

The section groups should next be arranged according to their intrinsic meaningful relationships with each other. The arrangements will be based upon the fundamental principles of dependability, purpose, need, values, functions, and forms. The groups should be harmonized and organized into a continuously interwoven and flowing network that must give satisfaction to the client(s) and end-users, as well as to the consultant.

This stage can be considered the second stage of spatial relationships, with the first being that achieved before the groupings. The importance attached to the proper and continuous flows necessitates the secondary attention given to the spatial relationships. The importance of this stage cannot be over emphasized, as it enables us to look deeper into the analysis of space to make sure that the spatial relationships are properly arranged in an acceptable sequence. For instance, if "group A" is more related in functions, needs, values, and inter-grouping activities with "group C" than with "group B," then "group A" must be arranged next to C and before B, and so on. Also if groups A, B and C need mutual access to each other for more effective activities, actions, usage, or flow, then these three groups must be interwoven with a common flow through an intersecting spatial link. A concept of "inside flowing out and outside flowing in" can be adopted in this situation to achieve collaborative functional actions, usage, or flow relationships among these interdependent groups.

Spaces should not be arranged in a mechanically sterile fashion. Instead, the spatial relationships must be softened and enlivened, always bearing in mind that we are creating these spaces for human beings. Therefore, the sociological and psychological aspects of spaces in human relationships must be considered. Research conducted with a group of mice harbored in a "city" made with cardboard papers to scale and using different colors, shapes and sizes, confirmed that the behavior pattern of the mice groups changed as they moved through and around the spaces. In some sections they were very moody and withdrawn. In other sections they appeared alternately excited, relaxed, and playful. The research was conducted to uncover how spaces, shapes, and forms can affect human behavior. It served to draw our attention to the importance of sociology in spatial arrangements, horizontally and vertically, and in the use of shapes and colors.

BRIEF COMPARISONS

It is always enriching to draw analytical comparisons from past, present, and future studies. In this way one can enhance the assignment at hand. A project must not be treated in isolation, as one must always bear in mind that human nature in general has overarching similarities, though with degrees of differences and variation. Therefore, after assembling the facts, the next most reasonable step is to compare and contrast the current project with other similar projects to harness the benefits of the past and accurately project into the future.

The process of comparative analogy must be self-driven and should radiate from an inward analysis of the brief's design and groupings as already developed by the consultant. Next, the analytical net should be spread wider, beyond the specific area of assignment.

One of the major reasons for this stage is to make sure that the project is not overreaching in its scope and development. Further, it must also be adequately inclusive of other alternatives that may be needed to enrich the assignment at hand. Comparative analysis enhances attendant standards and guides the mind to greater reasoning.

Comparative processes are utilized to have a clearer picture of the merits and drawbacks of the things that are arranged in comparison, and to discover hidden parts or silent elements of things previously presumed to be wholly understood.

CHAPTER 4

BRIEF DIAGRMMATIC
FORMATTING

At this stage, information gathering and analyses are complete and all is ready for the design of the project to begin. The mind at this point is activated and is ready to practicalize the theoretical imaginations. The brain is ready for an outflow. The big question now, therefore, is how to set the design process into motion.

First, in a diagrammatic format, one begins by arranging the brief according to functions and movement flows. See the illustration below:

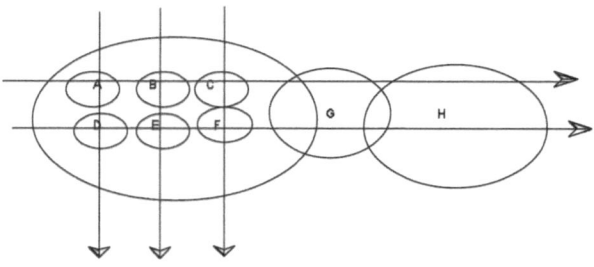

FIGURE 3

The diagram is arranged based on the findings of our "brief analysis." A must be meaningfully related to B; A to D; B to E; B to C; and C to F—all in a common master group that relates to G and G to H. In this way the flow is interwoven and continues seamlessly blending with the existing environment. At this point, it must be emphasized that projects do not exist in isolation. They form part of a wider arena, and therefore must blend, integrate, and flow into it to form part of it.

BREIF BUBBLING

This page contains the development of the brief, and it can be likened to the commencement of the growth of a fertilized egg in humans. The effective growth of the brief at this level is dependent on the aforementioned stages, particularly the last, which is shown in the brief diagram.

The entire process is like a series of chain links. Each link is closely joined with those adjacent to it, and each must communicate with the others for continuity and a good result. The mind that is already consumed with information and ideas is set to continue the flow from the diagram as illustrated in Figure 4, below:

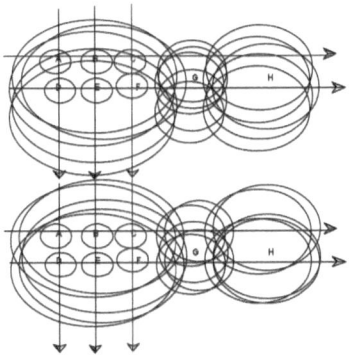

FIGURE 4

Figure 4, above, shows the launch of the bubbling process, and the way or method it is derived, through diagrammatic analysis. The flow should not be mechanical or superimposed, but must emanate from a process of continuity that is self creating.

The bubbling must not be forced to have a pattern, nor must it be required to take a particular direction. Instead, it can completely regenerate itself—especially if satisfaction is not forthcoming through the bubble movement already created. It must not have a presumed format. Further, alternative bubbles of master thinking can be created for comparative analysis and thereby enable the higher achievement of design fulfillment. See the illustrative diagram in Figure 5, below:

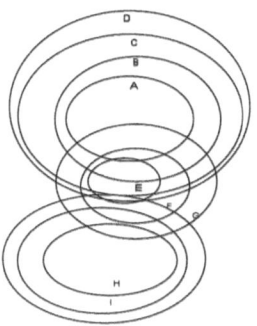

FIGURE 5

The diagram, above, reveals an alternative bubbling pattern that is spinning outwardly in a continuous format of flow.

Another bubbling alternative is illustrated in Figure 6, below:

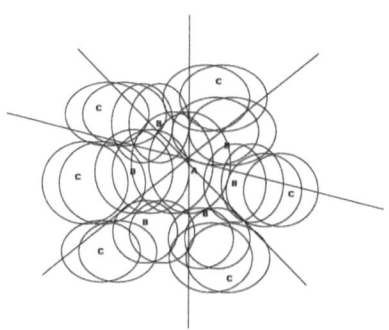

FIGURE 6

The bubbles in Figure 6, on page 18, originated from a central bubble and are continuously radiating, multiplying, growing, and expanding on different axes as they increase in size and form.

Throughout the bubbling process, the mind must not be constrained or limited. The pencil must be given absolute freedom to flow, and yet must be meaningfully guided by the brief-detailed analysis already established in the previous stages.

The brief bubbling stage is actually the "ideas mingling" level, and it is very important that we do not restrict the mind at this point, but let it keep bubbling. When any idea finally "clicks" or falls into place, the resulting registration generates a signal that will radiate all over and the brain will register satisfaction. Figure 7, below, is an illustration of another set of bubbles:

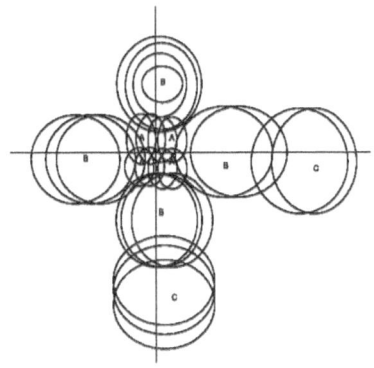

FIGURE 7

The bubbles, above, are moving along upon a North/South or East/West axis, multiplying and increasing as they bubble along.

Just like soap foaming naturally and effortlessly into bubbles, our bubbles must not be controlled. Instead, they should be allowed to create and re-create themselves and flow as naturally as possible until a final point of no return (i.e., a conclusion) is reached.

It is actually possible to go on and on into bubbles and bubbling, but the aforementioned illustrations will suffice at this point.

BUBBLING IN BUBBLE GROUPS

At this stage it is necessary to elevate the bubbling process to a new level, increasing and expanding it into other sections along the conceptual borders. The boundaries must be integrated to form a functionally flowing unit that is well articulated and perfectly interwoven into a great circulating, radiating unit with a common union of activities.

See the illustrative diagram, Figure 8, below:

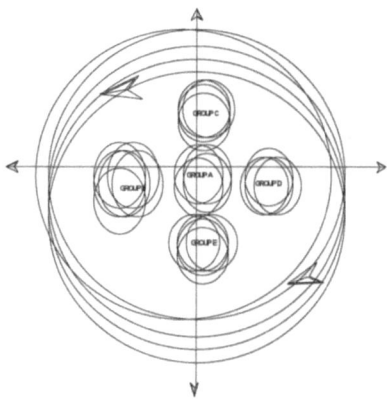

FIGURE 8

The Illustration in Figure 8, above, depicts a flowing relationship among bubbling groups. Again, the bubbling should not be restricted, but should be allowed to freely generate and multiply itself. There must be no barriers; in other words all barriers must be broken, allowing the mind to flow, albeit guided by the master brief analysis.

It is always advisable to keep creating alternatives during bubbling, as this will ultimately help in decision making. Once the bubbling creatively "clicks," an "acceptable" signal will register in the brain.

An illustrative diagram is provided in Figure 9, on the next page.

We must allow our mind to continuously bubble and juggle the analyzed brief until fulfillment or the desired quality of satisfaction is achieved.

FIGURE 9

The Illustration in Figure 9 is a multiple-group bubbling, revolving in a continuous circular and unifying movement around a central focal point.

Another series of bubblings in a bubble group can be seen in Figure 10, below.

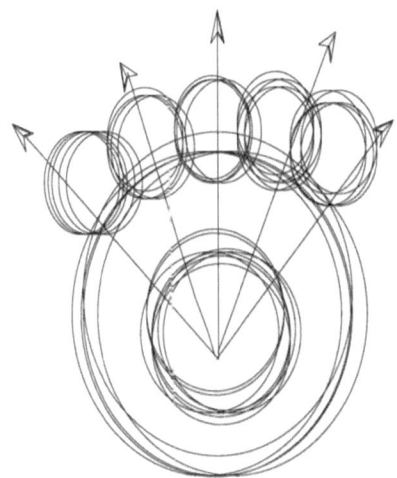

FIGURE 10

The Illustrative diagram above is a bubbling process that moves from an inner bubble to an outer bubble, and then radiates into multiple bubbles along the outer layer of the large bubble without losing a focus on the originating bubble.

A layman's mind may wonder about the meaning of all these endless bubbles, but a mind fixed and focused in a professional design orientation can derive considerable inspiration and direction from the aforementioned guidelines.

The illustrations of bubbling and bubbles, at this stage, are not drawn to scale. Further, they do not exist in perfect curves or circles. They are just multiples of continuous creation achieved by the free flowing movement of a pencil, guided by the translated, analyzed, and programmed master brief. The bubbles are grouped, compared, and diagrammatically allowed to flow into more elaborate bubble patterns, systematically tailored to achieve a unique masterpiece that will stand the test of time.

The interesting thing about this approach to design is that, when the professional consultant is well versed in his assignment, he is not copying a prefabricated model, but is rather achieving singular creativity from the fundamental principles of design tactics.

CHAPTER 5

ACTUALITY IN BUBBLES

PHASE 1

In Figures 1 and 2 we observed illustrative diagrams of the egg development of the Anopheles mosquito, and of the human zygote which attaches itself to the uterus wall and begins to grow and develop by cell division to form an embryo. In like manner, every successful creation must undergo a kind of metamorphosis before achieving a culminating end result.

At this stage, the bubbles are transforming and have advanced into "actuality in bubbles." The shapes are beginning to be defined. The pencil is sketching faster and constantly on the bubbles, while moving freely and uninterrupted as the shapes begin to emerge naturally. The mind must be free from any contrived attempt to define the shapes, and must instead allow unhindered movement of the pencil to determine the shapes emerging from the bubbles (see the illustrative diagram in Figure 11, below, for clarification):

FIGURE 11

The defining flow of the pencil should be allowed to wander from the outside perimeter walls of the bubbles to the inner perimeter walls of the bubbles without hindrance. In this way, the pencil is migrating and moving for discovery (see the illustrative diagram in Figure 12, below, for clarification):

FIGURE 12

The inward movement of the pencil further defines the shapes and gives new meaning to them. The pencil must continue to move until the bubbles are saturated and the emerging shapes are clearly defined.

The same process must be repeated for all the alternate bubbles that were created from the brief for the same assignment (or project). Through this stage we should have developed a number of these bubbles, constituting the first phase of "Actuality in Bubbles." The continuous and repeated movement of the pencil on the bubbles must not stop until all the spaces labeled or numbered for specific uses are clearly defined into meaningful shapes and patterns, while maintaining the originality of the brief translation, analysis, programming, groupings, group relationships, comparisons and diagrammatic interpretations, as already constituted.

See the illustrative diagram Figure 13, on the next page, for a second demonstration of bubbles to Actuality in Bubbles.

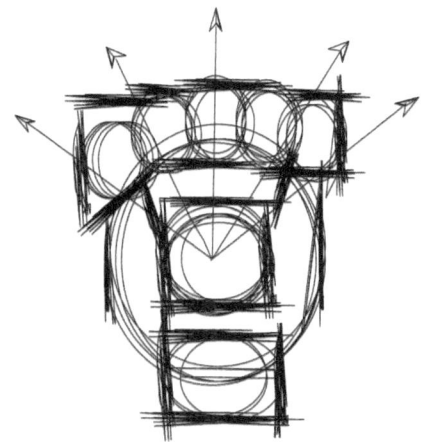

FIGURE 13

As shown in Figure 13, above, the orientation of the bubbling in bubbles contributes to the outcome of the Actuality in Bubbles—which constitutes "Phase 1." Further, Figure 11 is continued into Figure 12 as "Alternate 1" and into Figure 13 as "Alternate 2" of the same project. It is advisable to develop a few more alternates for secondary comparative studies before entering the next phase—Phase 2—of Actuality in Bubbles.

PHASE 2

At this stage, elements of scale are introduced into the Actuality in Bubbles. The best method for achieving this is by creating a scaled master grid in horizontal and vertical format in any of the following dimensions: 1 meter X 1 meter, or 2 meter X 2 meter, 3 meter X 3 meter, 4 meter X 4 meter grids as the case may be. At this juncture the Actuality in Bubbles becomes superimposed—Phase 1 on the formulated master-grid—and the pencil flow is once again recommenced in order to put the entire bubbled arrangements into scaled proportions.

We must still be guided by the analysis derived from the master brief, which must have clear spatial information on sizes, proportions, and the relationships of spaces to each other. This stage will gradually lead us to clearly define the necessary two dimensional scaled shapes before Actuality in Bubbles-Phase 3 begins (see the illustrative diagram Figure 14 for a demonstration of a master grid and how Actuality in Bubbles may flow to define patterns).

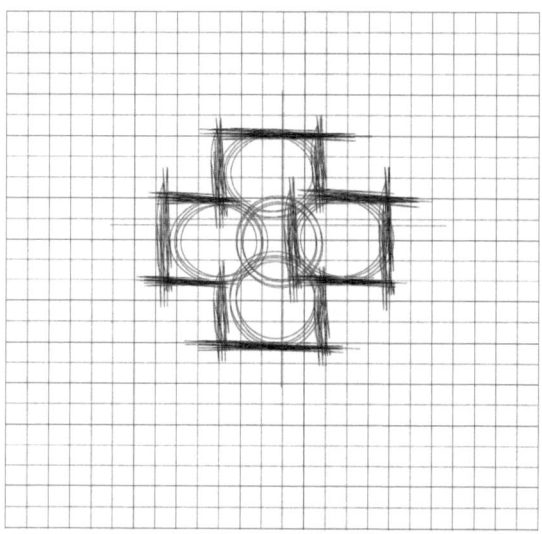

FIGURE 14

Figure 14, above, shows how the grid lines running horizontally and vertically serve to gradually guide, determine, and control spaces and shapes, and how they are also instrumental in appropriating proportions as derived from the master brief. We can take another example from "Bubbling in Bubble Groups," as illustrated in Figure 10, to demonstrate how we can achieve Actuality in Bubbles (see the illustrative diagram in Figure 15, on the next page).

The grid lines play a critical role in guiding the pencil at this stage. Some new shapes have been achieved from the bubbles developed in Figure 10. We must note that the axis orientation of the bubbles in Figure 10, when superimposed on the master

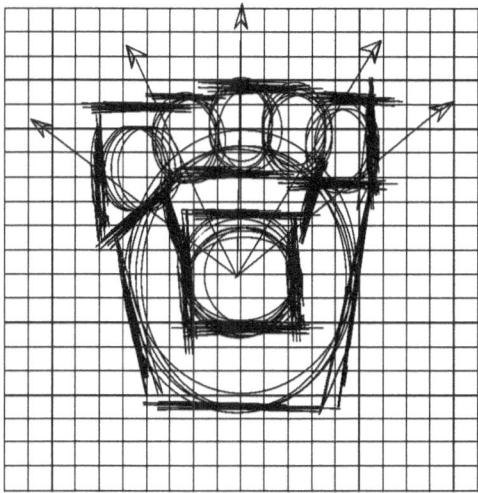

FIGURE 15

grid, will guide the directional flow of the pencil in constant and creative motion. The up and down and continuous chain-like movement of the pencil will define the shapes that best suit the bubbles.

The preceding methods will help us to generate as many alternatives as we may wish, which will in turn enable us to determine those most suitable for the project, after a rigorous design jury critiques and analyzes of all the available samples. The ultimately selected sample will then graduate into the next level.

PHASE 3

This phase can also be referred to as the Schematic Design Bubbling Phase. By this point, the available shapes have been defined, but they must be still guided by the master grid. This is the time to start brushing up the activity in the bubbles into schemes. The ideas are beginning to have shape, form, and meaning; but the meaning must be the answers to the client's brief, as translated by the consultant. The master brief is an examination questions, and at this stage the questions should have already been decoded, allowing the answers to begin flowing through the pencil. The definitive outcome of Actuality in Bubbles-Phase 2 must now be superimposed on a fresh master grid for commencement of Actuality in Bubbles-Phase 3 proper.

This stage is carefully guided by the detailed brief to make sure that all the information available is transformed graphically and complies with the bubbles and is trim-lined by our master grid. At this point, experience comes into play. However, while there is a growing sense of design independence, it is still necessary to comply with the rules as established by the guiding theorems and principles of bubbling in bubbles. For now we are in control, but the bubbles will come back again in another form to resume guidance of the project.

The design process can now be moved over to either the drawing board or the computer, as desired, in order to have a properly defined schematic master plan derived from the established bubbles scheme.

This point signifies the commencement of the detailed master plan flow-and-spaces-proportionality arrangements at the schematic or single-line level. Aesthetics, color separations, and all the ideas developed during the brief analysis, investigations, and research, and elaborated and diagrammatically captured through the programming level, will now be incorporated into the schematic development stage. As each incorporation occurs, the project will systematically graduate into the next stage on the progression ladder.

CHAPTER 6

BUBBLES IN
MULTIPLE DIMENSIONS

BUBBLES IN TWO DIMENSIONS

Shapes and actual sizes must be clearly defined; topography—that is, natural contours and conditions—will become a serious factor that should determine the next phase of shapes, forms, and characteristics of the developing concept that must emerge. These conditions will enhance and widen our creative imaginations; ideas will be elaborated in the mind on how to incorporate, improve, and enhance the gifts of the natural conditions inherent in the proposed area of development.

It is important to note that developing concepts must blend, integrate, and flow into the topography of any proposed development. Only through topographical harmony can the emerging concepts become part of and one with the natural conditions of that area. The result is uniqueness and a better flow of man and the activities of man and his creations.

Concepts must derive originality, form, and function from enduring gifts of nature to enhance the emerging conceptualizations. The natural conditions of a place must intertwine and resonate with the bubbles, blending them into the topography of the area while also maintaining all bubbled characteristics of the brief as translated. These will then give rise to bubbles in two (2) dimensions, which will launch the flow of development into the next arena.

BUBBLES IN THREE DIMENSIONS

Practicality will now come into play at this point. It is highly recommended that all bubbles in two (2) dimensions should be translated into three (3) dimensional study models. In this way it will be possible to feel the relationship of forms within the natural environment.

At this point, the forms can be depicted in block format to represent the derived spaces in scale. The models, superimposed on the natural environment, should be free to juggle upside-down and inside-out repeatedly and continuously within the parameters of the master brief. It must be noted that each level of successful juggling should be closely studied, analyzed, and understood. No hurried conclusions should be drawn at this stage of schematic bubbles analysis in three dimensional models. Ideally, this activity should be fun, and the designer must try as much as possible to enjoy this explorative experience with the models in order to maximize the creative benefits of the exercise.

Many different sets of three dimensional study models should be created and manipulated. This stage can be interpreted as the "toy stage," as it involves creative play with the models in toy-like forms. Ideally, the designer will constantly change the shape, position, pattern, and arrangement of the models, and sometimes completely change everything altogether to fully appreciate each model from numerous different perspectives. Just as children often become carried away in playing with their toys, so must the designer become completely involved in the joy, excitement, and optimum appreciation of creation. It must be noted that this process of evaluation, analysis, and critique of the three dimensional models being juggled around must not stop until the brain "clicks" for satisfaction, signaling acceptance of the form, function, and arrangement.

The three dimensional models can be made or constructed from any material that is comfortable to work with, including cardboard papers, strawboard papers, balsa wood—in fact, anything that can be used to achieve three dimensional shapes. At this stage, undue attention should not be paid to the superficial details of the assembled bubbles in schematic format. Rather, the designer should concentrate on the geometric forms and the topography of the area of assignment.

The designer should keep moving the three dimensional forms around the designated areas of assignment until an alignment is achieved that will be in harmony with the natural conditions of the master brief. Effective assessment will involve a focus on horizontal and vertical details, relationships of the forms, and the suitability of the forms to the available topography.

The designer must ensure that all ideas are completely exhausted with model creations and the juggling of the emerging shapes and forms. Ultimately, the designer will know when a point of no-return has been reached, and this will signal the time to end the experiment with study models and schematic analysis. Then the time will have arrived to decide on the final forms acceptable for the drive toward optimal conceptualization.

Upon achieving satisfaction, the next target will be the blending of the accepted forms in all ramifications. This will include, but not be limited to, vertical and horizontal flow and function harmonizations, which will lead the way to the next level of development.

CHAPTER 7

BUBBLES TO SHAPES

Transforming bubbles into shapes requires a return to the drawing board for proper details of space, dimensions, and integration of all accepted forms. This level requires the addition of touch-ups, blending, and the enrichment of ideas, resulting in the development and refinement of conceptual bubbles into definite shapes. At this level, all acceptably defined bubbles must be configured to scale in readiness for section analysis and development. Section analysis will help in the study and understanding of the relationships of the bubbles in two dimensions to the ultimate bubbles in three dimensions, culminating in the Actuality in Bubbles.

The sections, cut from the longitudinal and latitudinal aspects of critical areas of the project, will help lend greater understanding to the arrangement of the forms through detailed analysis.

Analysis of the sections will help the designer to digest the vertical flow and functional interrelationships and coherency. In this way the designer is able to meaningfully readjust, modify, and/or agree with the new developments as arranged. Study models can be cut open to create three dimensionally sectioned effects for better comprehension of the inner arrangements of the spaces. This must occur before any final conclusions can be drawn regarding the best way to transform the bubbles to shapes. Only after the sectional analysis can the proposed shapes, forms, and spatial arrangements be accepted and adopted for creating the design scheme through human creative metamorphosis.

At this juncture, the designer is now poised to gather, organize, arrange, harmonize, and overhaul the entire scheme and assemble the components together to form a unique creation. It is now becoming a product of diligent endeavor, guided by the fundamental tenets of design theorems and concepts metamorphosed to produce an entirely unique concept. These applications, as described here, can be keyed and channeled to achieve the enhanced development of critical elements of urban design.

CHAPTER 8

UNDERSTANDING URBAN DESIGN FOR BUBBLES

The principles of bubbling in bubbles for conceptualization are applicable to most creative design professions, but the "manner" of the profession must be understood before the theorems can be readily applied.

The profession of Urban Design evolved as a child of necessity within the university curricula in the 1950s. However, it must be noted that in practicality it had always existed, albeit silently, throughout recorded history—people and their activities have always shaped habitable environments.

As a profession, it swings between architecture and planning, and is mostly concerned with larger scale arrangements and the designing of cities. Consequently, its focus is on the formation and organization of buildings and the space relationships between them, but not with the actual designing of the individual buildings.

Ideologically, architecture functions within the realm of urban design and the later within the realm of planning. All three are truly not separable, but collaboratively aim toward a common goal for humanity for today and tomorrow. Therefore, each must be viewed from an overarching "aerial" or holistic point of view.

The architecture must be designed to accommodate the designated zoning areas and building ordinances, as dictated by the master urban design plan. The latter deals with the city in parts, as allocated by city planning. The three professions are integrated, functioning at different frequencies but towards a common general agenda.

Urban design is mostly concerned with broad spectrum, long term projections for development, such as neighborhoods, re-settlements, and city re-creation—as opposed to individual projects involving only a few years (i.e., 1, 2, or 3 years) for development, such as a single multi-storey building in architecture. At the larger, integrated development scale, planners must consider multiple conditions and uses, including: climate, pedestrian orientation, neighborhood composition and identity, and forms and patterns of transportation used.

URBAN DESIGN STRATEGIES

Each city has its peculiarities and problems, and all are anchored in a general collection of common characteristics that can be approached by way of the following basic phases and/or sub-phases used in urban planning and design:

1. Detailed Study
   a. Data organization
   b. Memory map
   c. Itemization of expansion and non-expansion zone-sand useful details
2. Combination of ideas
3. Assessment
4. Carrying Out Decisions

Each of these urban planning and design phases and sub-phases are further elaborated and detailed below.

1. Detailed Study
   a. *Data Organization:* This sub-phase utilizes the primary working concepts for an assignment, which include topography, population, transportation, land use, and natural systems. It is also important to understand the site conditions, the neighborhoods, and the business areas.

These will help in analyzing:

    i.   The adequacy of the natural condition of the soil for proposed use.

    ii. The relationship of traffic to population.

    iii. The proportion of land to population.

    iv. The necessary public utilities.

    v.   Subdivision ordinances and zoning regulations.

    vi. Open spaces, institutions, and parking conditions.

    vii. The financial standing of the area

b. *Memory Map:* A "Memory Map," or "Visual Map" as it is popularly branded by urban designers, is the "memory image" of a city as derived from walking around in it. The Memory Map is used to better understand the orientation of structures and spaces within a city. Various symbols can be used to characterize and identify the key elements and important sections and boundaries encountered, thereby depicting them in a graphic format for others to more quickly and completely understand. We can also use a Memory Map to analyze the pedestrian distances between different areas.

c. *Itemization of Expansion and Non-expansion Zones:* Constant change is a common characteristic that may not easily be accommodated in cities and their zones. Therefore, the urban designer must itemize the expandable and non-expandable areas in order to accommodate growth and change. The expandable (soft areas) are those areas that can still accommodate growth, either by virtue of vacancies or via reclamation from nature. The non-expandable (hard) areas are those sections that cannot absorb growth due to rigid restrictions, such as areas bounded by cemeteries, bodies of water, etc.

d. *Practical and Useful details:* This sub-phase involves a study and incorporation of our findings to the design in practical terms, understanding the relationships between movements of land-users and their effect on the prevailing circulation patterns. Analysis in three dimensions is necessary to formulate meaningful solutions.

2. *Combination of Ideas:* The gathering of ideas will illuminate the constraints of various problems, and suggest necessary solutions. These will form the basic input for the generation of the brief analysis, programming, groupings, comparisons, diagrammatic illustrations, and the bubbling through to conceptualization. Proper brief translation is important to highlight fundamental problems—especially those associated with housing areas, such as inherent conflicts between vehicular traffic and pedestrian movements—to determine the best solutions considering the financial implications to the client(s).

3. *Assessment:* Assessment must be continuous and can be grouped into stages, the first being to compare the technical solutions available to the problems existing and then evaluating each for the likelihood of client(s) and public acceptance. The second is assessing the degree of solutions achieved within the overall context of the proposal, and making sure that they fit the existing problems and can be effectively implemented.

4. *Carrying Out Decisions:* Land-use controls and capital expenditures are the primary methods of implementing urban design proposals, and they include, among others, zoning ordinances. Zoning ordinances can be enacted to realize the proposal and could be sub-divided into two parts:
   i. First, the map (and design proposals) must be sufficiently and satisfactorily detailed for easy identification of parcels of land in a particular zone.
   ii. Second, the details about the type of development that may be carried out in a given zone must be understood, and the proposed use clause must be applicable to the zone. Some specified items on the ordinance include among others:

a. *Site layout requirements*

—Minimum plot size

—Minimum setbacks of buildings to front, side, or rear of the plot

—Width and length of plots

—Maximum developable percentage of plot that may be covered by structures

—Fence requirements

b. *Building characteristics requirements*

—Maximum height

—Maximum number of floors

—Maximum floor area

c. *Use clause*:

—Specifying number of families for residential zones and what is considered a family.

—Categories and types of non-residential uses allowed in the zone (for example, churches, mosques, and professional offices).

—Commercial zones where applicable ordinances will make it clear what types of use are permitted and those not allowed.

d. *Procedural Matters*

—Determinations that specify the approval processes necessary to guarantee the conformity of all plans submitted for approval and building permits to the relevant zoning ordinances.

Guiding principles for determining satisfactory urban design solutions include:

i.   Good flow of interwoven arrangement of spaces and zones

ii. Proper separation or reduced clash of vehicular traffic with pedestrians

iii. Barriers against weather and noise.

iv. Good functional relationships between land users.

v. Adequate relaxation spaces, properly landscaped.

vi. Easy flow of people.

A ROAD VIEW OF PART OF PARIS, FRANCE
A good separation of pedestrians with vehicular traffic as
shown in the illustration, above .

A SECTION OF AMSTERDAM, HOLLAND
A sectional view of Amsterdam, Holland (including canal,
pedestrian, and vehicular traffic arrangements).
The view depicts a good separation of movement, with canals
running parallel to roads, pedestrians, and shuttle trains in the
downtown area of Amsterdam, Holland.

CHAPTER 9

PLANNING IN VIEW FOR BUBBLES

The growth in human activities and settlements, requiring interconnectivity, advancement in various sectors, and the need for the easy flow of people and vehicles—plus the necessity to accommodate expansion—make it mandatory to plan for the future.

The type of development in any given land area will affect the volume of traffic within and around the zone. Further, the use to which the land is put will also affect air pollution, noise levels, water availability, and the socioeconomic nature of the area. The vast and sophisticated conditions of human development amply confirm the need for the planning discipline, both as a profession and as a function of organized institutions. Urban planning is essential for the formulation of development guidelines, ordinances, polices, and implementation processes.

Quality advance planning will ensure the proper and orderly provision of essential amenities and services, such as water, gas, electricity, waste disposal, transportation, education, public safety, recreation, police and fire protection. From the above facts it becomes obvious that urban planning is an essential function of government, or an agency appointed and authorized to perform planning duties according to approved guidelines.

Planning is grouped as follows: 1) the development and/or re-designing of master plans; 2) zoning-related issues; and, 3) environment impact analyses and research.

In developing master plans, planners must ensure a proper pattern of expansion in order to maintain or improve associated land-use values. A system of development must be utilized that enhances access to facilities such as shopping centers, schools, and relaxation areas. A well-integrated road network must be arranged for the maintenance of efficient traffic flows. The functions and activities of spaces should be carefully evaluated before proximity to each other is permitted. For example, high quality planning will define and separate pedestrian and bicycle traffic from automobile traffic.

Planning is also concerned with the preservation and improvement of existing spaces and structures. Therefore, laws may be enacted for preserving historic institutions.

Economic development may also be a concern for urban planners. Quality planning can facilitate the conditions necessary to help revive existing industries and contribute to favorable conditions for professional establishments.

Another area that falls under the jurisdiction of planners is the environmental impact assessment and analysis. It could positively or negatively affect the planning process, depending upon the factors requiring consideration in calculating opportunity costs.

Planning is in the public interest, both in the short run and the long run. It seeks to solve problems by way of anticipation, and also proposes solutions for those already at hand. The long term nature inherent in the implementation of planning may sometimes result in only partial compliance, or it may require repeated alterations, which could be frustrating to the planner.

It is important to acknowledge that there is always a political undertone to planning, and a planner must learn to accommodate this in order to participate in the profession. The complex nature of planning calls for diversity, versatility, and a sharp focus, which makes the profession both rewarding and unique.

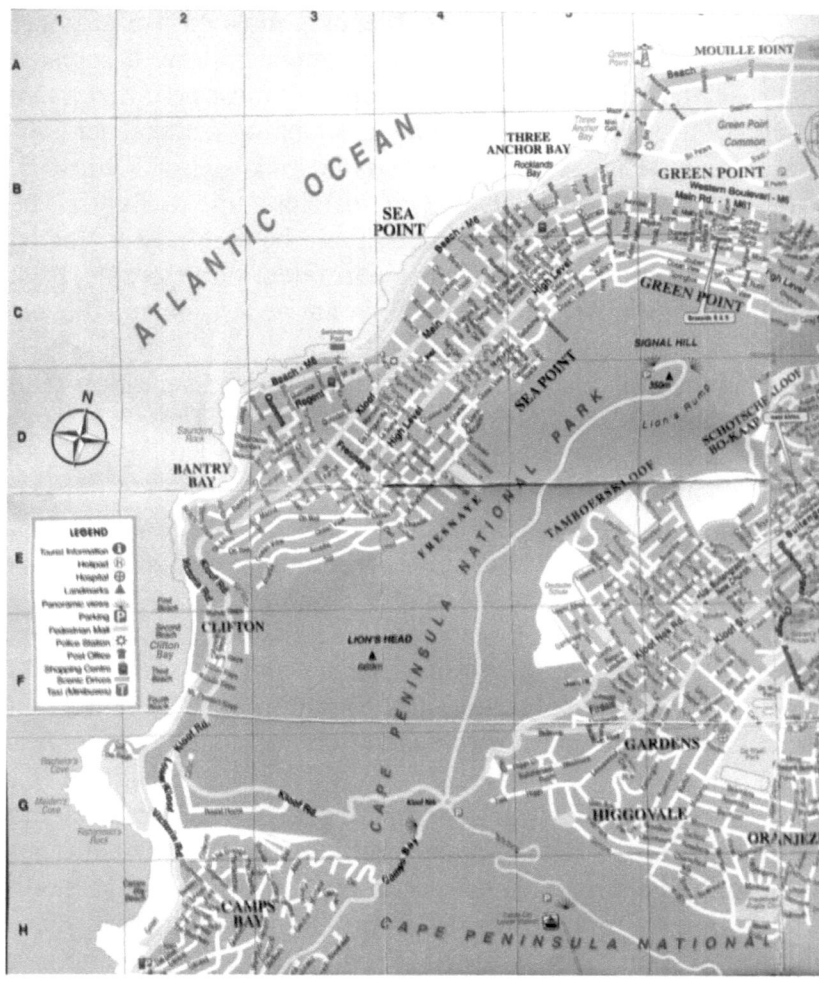

A MAP OF CAPE TOWN, SOUTH AFRICA FOR PLANNING ANALYSIS.
The planning concept as shown in the above map collaborated well with nature to achieve good values in habitation, relaxation, and tourism. The town has the Atlantic Ocean as a boundary on one side, and is partially conceptualized around another gift of nature: the Cape Peninsula National Park. The result is an outstanding urban-nature combination, where nature is enjoyed and appreciated in almost every direction.

BEACH DRIVE, CAPE TOWN, SOUTH AFRICA
A Beach Road drive in Cape Town reveals many advantages
of the natural gifts of nature made available through enhanced
planning.

STREET GUIDE MAP OF ABUJA, NIGERIA

AERIAL GEOGRAPHICAL MAP OF ABUJA AND ENVIRONS

HILLS AROUND ABUJA

AERIAL VIEW OF A SECTION OF ABUJA, NIGERIA

VIEW FROM ZUMA ROCK, ABUJA, NIGERIA

VIEW FROM MILLENNIUM PARK, ABUJA, NIGERIA

VIEW FROM NATIONAL ASSEMBLY, ABUJA, NIGERIA

VIEW FROM MILLENNIUM PARK IN ABUJA, NIGERIA

Abuja, the capital of Nigeria, is a modern and growing city. It is endowed with scattered hills and valleys that partially encircle the city. Urban planners capitalized on the topography of the surrounding countryside by conceiving and building a ring road around Abuja. The ring road serves as the link from the neighboring satellite towns and distribution into the city. Abuja is zoned into different use sections, with interwoven mixed use concept in almost all the zones. The adopted concept virtually eliminated the downtown city centre format, which allows for outward and inward radiation/distribution from the centre to all axis.

However, the planners did not take full advantage of the various gifts of nature to create holiday points, relaxation and recreational centers, and tourist attractions. In fact, the natural endowments were not satisfactorily incorporated with the city to any meaningful degree. Inside out and outside in—a flowing concept—could have been adopted to take full advantage of the remarkable topography. In spite of the oversight, considerable remedy is still possible. As a growing city, the current development plan can still be modified to provide the city with world class planning status for both the inhabitants and tourists alike. Bubbles to Conceptualization is a vital theorem for great imaginations, and could be put to fruitful use in this situation.

CHAPTER 10

CONCLUSION

BUBBLES TO CONCEPTUALIZATION

The major thrust of this book is to formulate and reactivate theorems that will serve as guiding lights in the creative process. The theorems presented can accelerate the creative mind toward developing concepts that are unique and original. In this way, the process of thinking through trends, topography, culture, sociology, psychology, and functionality can be enhanced. Further, the issues of environmental impact, science, and technology are also optimally addressed. All are blended together in a transformative process that emulates the gifts of nature (i.e., via embryo-bubbles). In this way, designers and planners can arrive at solutions that will stand the test of time even while incorporating the concepts derived from the master brief.

Bubbles to concept theorems are applicable to all designers and planning professionals in the field of architecture, landscape architecture, and urban design and planning.

Obviously, bubbles' theorems, like most theorems, can readily "click" for a creative professional, provided the expert is well informed on the particular profession or has a good understanding of the profession. Otherwise, application of the theorem may not easily "flow" from technical concepts to creative outcomes.

The Bubbles to Concept goes back to the roots of the assignment, before moving through the brief stage to translation, analysis, programming, groupings, groupings relationships, comparisons, diagrammatic illustration, bubbling, bubbling in

Bubbles Groups, Actuality in Bubbles, bubbles in two dimensions, bubbles in three dimensions, Bubbles to Shapes, and finally concluding in Bubbles to Conceptualization.

As already discussed, it won't be possible to diagnose a brief without being well versed on the information in the brief. Neither can one translate a language they don't speak, or analyze information they don't understand, or write a program without knowledge of the format, and so on.

Therefore, it is correct to say that the Bubbles theorems for design conceptualization are presented for use by professionals in practice, or at least in active training.

The theorems are tailored to blend into any of the fields identified above. In planning, they are used to understand the brief clearly and properly, before plotting the brief into the theorem.

Unquestionably, these theorems will help professionals to achieve originality that is "trendy" in terms of time and technology. This is accomplished by ensuring the good flow of spaces, pedestrians, and vehicular traffic, while creating a city that will radiate in function and flow, and optimize the comfort of its inhabitants and tourists.

SELECTED BIBLIOGRAPHY

G. O. Eweluwa, G. A. Odunze, A. C. Anozie; Revision Integrated Science For JSC Examinations. Revised Edition (African First Publishers Plc.).

John M. Levy, Contemporary Urban Planning,

Pearson International Edition, Eight Edition, Pearson Education International.

J. Nwokeji, Urban—Planning—Architecture—Studios (Library), case studies 1982 - 2009.

www.ingramcontent.com/pod-product-compliance
Lightning Source LLC
Chambersburg PA
CBHW030534290526
45786CB00004B/1717